ART MY WAY!

My First Art Portfolio!

M. RENEE VOGT

ART MY WAY!
MY FIRST ART PORTFOLIO!

iUniverse books may be ordered through booksellers or by contacting:

iUniverse
1663 Liberty Drive
Bloomington, IN 47403
www.iuniverse.com
844–349–9409

Because of the dynamic nature of the Internet, any web addresses or links contained in
this book may have changed since publication and may no longer be valid. The views
expressed in this work are solely those of the author and do not necessarily reflect the
views of the publisher, and the publisher hereby disclaims any responsibility for them.

Any people depicted in stock imagery provided by Getty Images are models,
and such images are being used for illustrative purposes only.
Certain stock imagery © Getty Images.

ISBN: 978–1–6632–4205–1 (sc)
ISBN: 978–1–6632–4207–5 (e)

Library of Congress Control Number: 2022912312

Print information available on the last page.

iUniverse rev. date: 07/06/2022

To: Artists's Assistant (Parents)

I have designed this book for you to enjoy with your child. Sit back and watch as they create beautiful artwork by using the guided line paper we used as children to learn our letters. In my over 40 years of experience in the art world, I have learned that when we look at an object they would like to draw, we can often become intimidated by it. However, if we learn to break that image down into shapes and fit together, almost like a puzzle, it makes it easier for us to understand the object. During my teaching experience, I have found students learn to draw more precisely learning to draw shapes and placing together instead of learning to draw line to line. This is their first portfolio. Watch how they improve from their first drawing to the next. I did everything in this book freehanded. I want students to look at characters and understand that simple and imperfect can still be beautiful!

To: Artist's (Students)

Enjoy learning how to break objects down visually into shapes and putting them together to learn to draw amazing artwork. Remember, lines don't have to be perfectly straight and circles don't have to be perfectly round to create beautiful artwork. Use the lined paper to help guide your drawings. Don't give up! Your next piece of art will be more beautiful than your first. Practice and have fun. Relax and draw it how you see it. Any questions at all, email me at rcc1616@gmail.com.

This is the Art Portfolio of:_____

5 Different Types of Shading to use when Drawing.

(Fish)   Parallel Hatching

(Bunny)   Contour Hatching

(Gecko)   Cross Hatching

(Bird)   Stippling

(Rhino)   Woven Hatching

Practice Shading Techniques on this Page.

Trace my lines on the next page to see how to assemble the Elephant

Title of your work:
Date:
Description:
Medium:

4

Let's Be Positive as we draw a BEE!

Title of your work:
Date:
Description:
Medium:

Let's have a Whale of a time drawing this character!

Title of your work:
Date:
Description:
Medium:

Puff out your cheeks as you draw this Puffer Fish!

Title of your work:
Date:
Description:
Medium:

Hope your fingers don't get sore when you draw this Dinosaur!

Title of your work:
Date:
Description:
Medium:

Don't fall asleep when you are drawing this SHEEP!

Title of your work:
Date:
Description:
Medium:

Let's **add a** Horn to make a Unicorn!

Title of your work:
Date:
Description:
Medium:

Have fun drawing this yuppy Puppy!

Title of your work:
Date:
Description:
Medium:

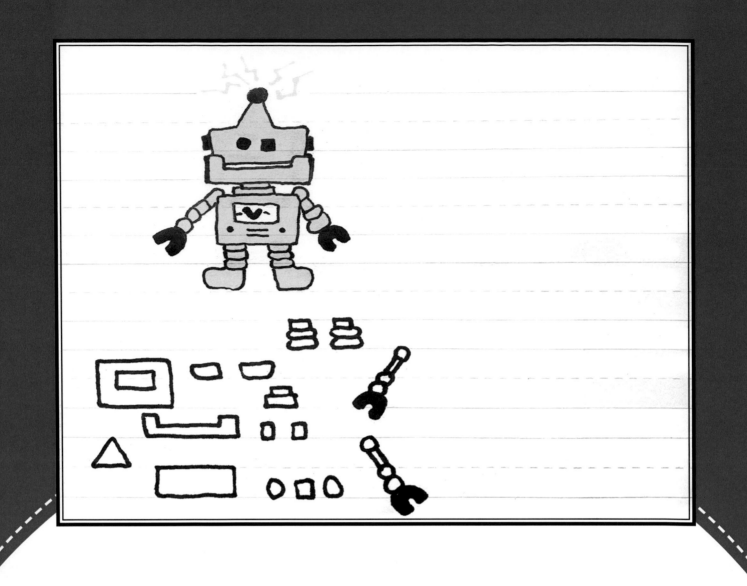

Dance a Beep Bop, when you draw this Robot!

Title of your work:
Date:
Description:
Medium:

You will be smitten once you draw this Kitten!

Title of your work:

Date:

Description:

Medium:

On your own, Break down this Lion and Crab.
What Shapes make up each character?